Beloved Words 2

Coloring Book
&
Devotion

Illustrated by
Heidi McKee

Devotions written by
various authors

Scripture breathed by
God the Father

Meet the Authors

So excited to bring you the second Beloved Words Coloring book! This time the pages are not only filled with pages you can color and meditate on God's word, but great applications as well. These stories are written by some amazing saints and I cannot wait to share who they are!

Marty McKee- my "shnookems", best friend and lover for 17 years! This man is the poster boy for dad, husband, servant! He has studied at Dallas Seminary and has a M.A. in Christian Education. He works there now helping others in their studies to know, teach and live God's Word. I am blessed to be his wife!

Tammy Grinn- my sister, my example is a mother of five. She has a house of teenagers with everyone going in opposite directions, but she always finds the solid middle and focus on Him! She and Matt have been married 16 years and you can follow her journey on her blog grinn.org

Karen Klein- My blessed Mother. It was a no brainer asking her to share a story about joy. This woman has continually blessed me and many others with written words of encouragement, joyous affirmations and spot on correction. She and my father, Randy, have been married 45 years and have 8 grandkids. Mom serves gladly in church and ministers by playing the piano beautifully.

Tammy White- my best friend and business partner for the past 8 years. This mom of four and wife to a full-time pastor is the easiest person to be friends with. She is loving, kind, and more compassionate than anyone I've ever met. We have grown a lot in striving to be a mom-serving HIM in the hard times.

Mary Ann Mardis- Friend and supporter. Mary Ann is happily married to Brad for 18 years now. She is a mom of a 13 y/o daughter and a 7 y/o son. She is a nurse and recently celebrated 20 years at Mercy Hospital in Oklahoma City. The Lord has recently brought our paths back together after 20 years as we have embarked on similar journeys, chasing hard after God's own heart.

Mary Beth Nix- Friend and fellow mom. Mary Beth and I met at Bible study at our kid's school. I quickly fell in love with her and KNEW she has God-wisdom to share. She is raising six amazing Godly people and serving her husband for nearly 24 years. Stay tuned for more of her MammaNix stories on an upcoming blog.

Heidi McKee- I am so blessed to be celebrating 17 years of marriage and raising my three precious kids. I've spent the last decade building a great team and direct sales business, and priding in the relationships I've made. My own personal quiet time of "doodling" in my Bible has transpired into a love for coloring God's word. So blessed to have 2 coloring books published now. I pray you find joy in coloring these pages and drawing closer to His amazing grace. For more information about my first book: _Finding your Passionate Purpose: In Life, Love and Leadership_. It is my goal and desire to help others find their God-given purpose and live it well!

These Pages have not been digitally enhanced.

The artwork is completely free-hand and one of-a-kind originals.

Try one yourself!

~

The Fear of the Lord
Proverbs 1:7

"The fear of the Lord is the beginning of knowledge, but fools despise wisdom and instructions." Proverbs 1:7

"The fear of the Lord is to hate evil; I hate pride and arrogance, evil behavior and perverse speech" Proverbs 8:13

These recent generations have a hard time showing true respect, let alone reverence. I believe this proverbs speak to that. When we show a true astonishment to God and what He is able to do, we begin to see things a little differently. To be wise, we start by understanding how Holy, how Perfect and how truly Amazing He is. When we understand this, we begin to hate evil all the more.

God, Creator of this universe, is beyond comprehension. He could smite us in one blow. He could wipe us from the Earth in one fell swoop—and according to scripture has done this once before. Why then do we let our sinful nature cloud our respect for that Awe-inspiring Father God? He alone gives us our breath!

To fear the Lord is an intentional act and one we must practice and teach to our children. This is the only way we will ever gain true wisdom. Without wisdom we will never understand the depth of the sacrificial love He has given.

Father God, you are amazing. Help me know that, remember that and ponder that as I bow before you King of kings and Lord of lords. You alone are worthy of my praise and my actions. Thank you for loving despite my lack of respect sometimes. Amen

Heidi McKee
Heidimckeeministries.com

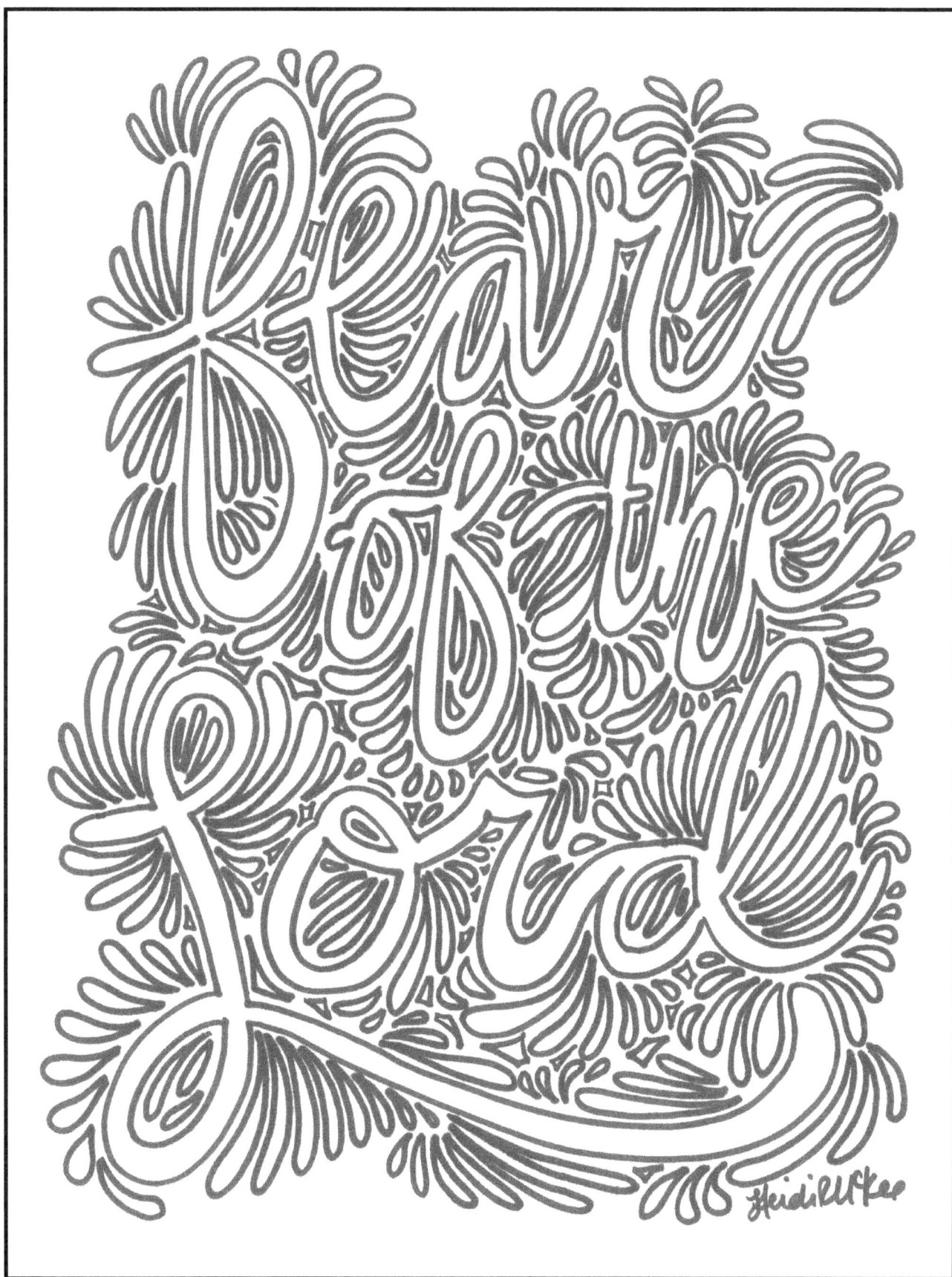

Have a Servant Heart
Matthew 20:28

If you have ever read books about leadership or heard speakers talk about leadership, it is highly likely you've heard the term "servant leadership". In most aspects this seems to be an oxymoron. One may think leadership is from the front like a drum major waving his baton leading his band. To think of a leader becoming less than or "below" the ones he leads feels wrong somehow. The truth is, however, that true leaders are those who are selfless and want more for the people they lead than they do for themselves.

Maybe you have had a teacher, coach, or someone who would stay up past bedtime and go out of her way to push you to be successful. Maybe it was a parent? How many times has your mom forfeited the last swig of milk or even the last donut? How many times did she come pick you up at midnight when she'd rather be snug in bed? We all know someone who has displayed true servant leadership. They handle the behind the scenes "get no glory" kind of acts which always highlights their servant leadership.

In first grade my daughters had a reading challenge. They had to read all year long to hit a goal and when they made it they could participate in a great big celebration. It was the "prom" of first grade and every one strived to achieve this great accomplishment. This task was difficult for savvy readers and almost impossible for struggling ones. So when my daughter's classmate, "Johnny", worked extra, hard people took notice. My daughter came home exclaiming over how many books "Johnny" had read! "Mom, he worked harder than ever!" She noticed.

The party came and "Johnny" woke up with a fever. It was totally devastating for him and I know it completely broke his heart. Even his classmates at the party felt the void of this hard worker – especially his teacher. Mrs. McCoy is a servant leader. She comes early, stays late and never complains. She loved those students like her own and truly wanted to see them succeed.

Although Mrs. McCoy has three kids and a busy schedule herself, she gathered snacks, mementos and party favors and at 3:45pm drove to "Johnny's" house. She brought the party to HIM! Balloons, streamers and celebration came knocking at his front door.

The only way others knew about this gesture is when he returned to school the next day. Grinning from ear to ear, he shared how much Mrs. McCoy loved him and wanted him to be a "super reader"!

It's important to stay observant because stories like that happen all the time. Visiting "Johnny" after school hours will NOT give her a raise or a bonus. It won't even make "Johnny" smarter, but it will show the other students that she cares more about them than she does for herself. WOW, I want to serve like that!

It is impossible to talk about servant leadership without mentioning Jesus. As the son of God, He came to this sinful world not only to share God's love, but to demonstrate a sacrificial kind of love. He even said, "I did not come to be served but to serve." The fact that the man who made the Heavens and Earth wanted to heal the sick, fix hearts or cry with the wounded blows my mind! He didn't come demanding a crown or a mansion, nor an endorsement – he simply came to serve. Daily I pray to serve like that.

Heidi McKee (excerpt from *Finding your Passionate Purpose*)

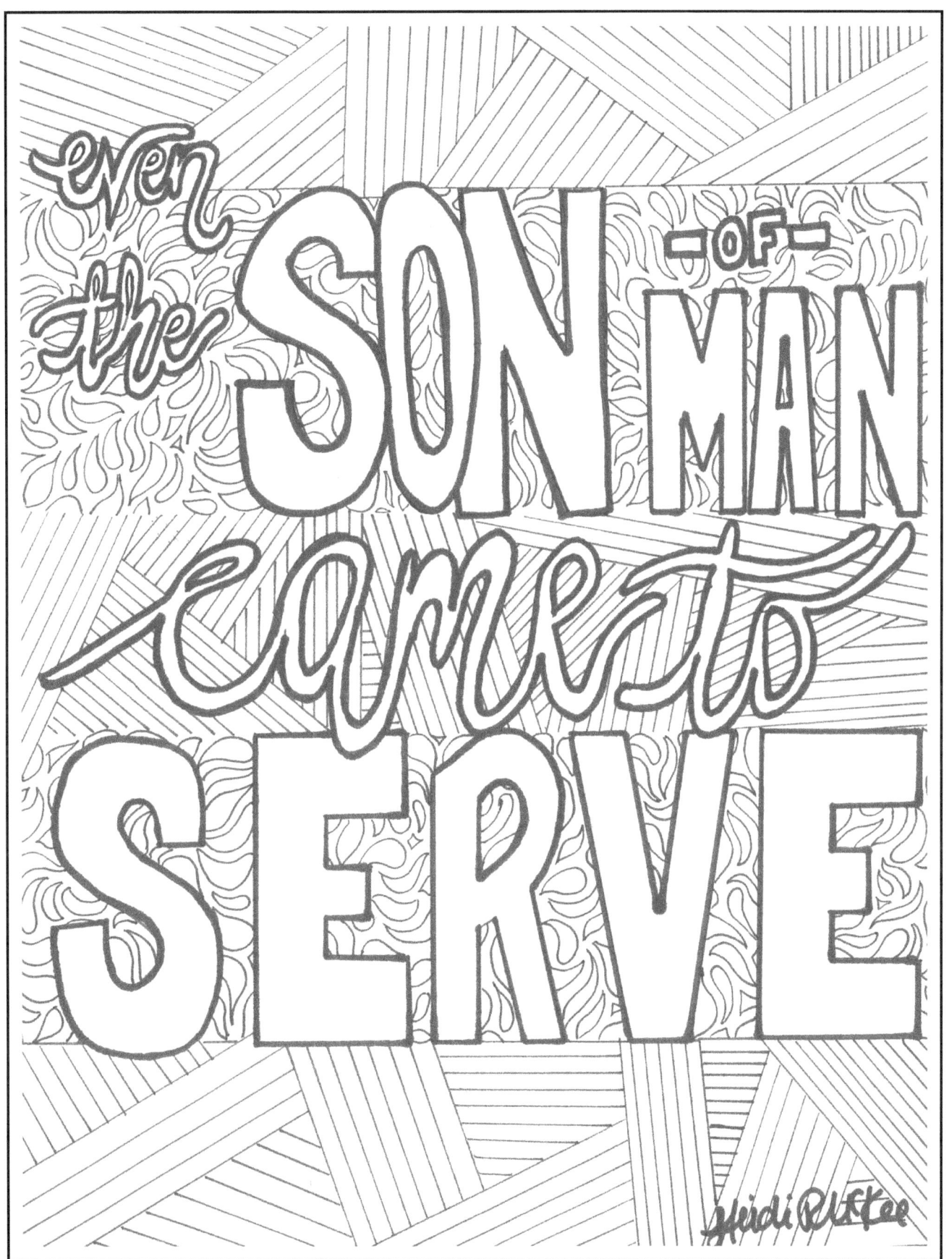

All Have Sinned
Colossians 3:23

"I'm not as bad as *that* guy" or "I don't steal or murder" are phrases I hear all the time when talking about the sinful nature of man. The sad, but true statement is that most people do not realize that we are sinful. Our flesh is inherently bad. According to scripture, ALL have sinned and ALL fall short of God's glory. (Col. 3:23) The first step is admitting that. Who wants to be a self-proclaimed offender? Who wants to be labeled a sinner? I know I don't! But it is true! Scripture is clear that we are born sinners: "Surely I was sinful at birth, sinful from the time my mother conceived me." Psalm 51:5

BUT, "I never cheated on my husband"...."I've never hit anyone"... right? How do you tell a really nice guy that he indeed is a sinner? This is what I've learned...

Most people know the 10 commandments and usually understand that when they break the 10 commandments it's not a good thing. To prove my point, you do not have to go any further than the first 3. 1) Make God #1 in your life. (um, yea guilty of breaking that one). 2) Do not worship any other idols. (ok, so that's hard to explain because in our culture everything is an idol but we do not even realize it.) 3) Do not lie. (boom. That's it, 100% sure we have all lied! EVEN if it was a healthy white lie to protect someone's feelings! Lied- you are separated from God. YUCK.

We are separated from a perfect and holy God. Because of His holiness, we are not worthy to be in his presence. But here is the kicker: HE MADE A WAY! He bridged the gap by taking our punishment! Jesus stood in our place so that we can spend eternity with the One who made us and loves us. When we admit we are a sinner and accept the gift He gave us then we have eternity to Thank Him!

Daily I sin, it's true, but daily Jesus forgives me and covers me with His loving forgiveness.

Thank you Father for your sacrifice on my behalf! Yes, I am a sinner, among the worse, yet you see grace! I am overwhelmed with gratitude and I want to spend my life showing it to you! Thank you for your undeserved mercy and grace. In Jesus name, Amen.

Heidi McKee
Heidimckeeministries.com

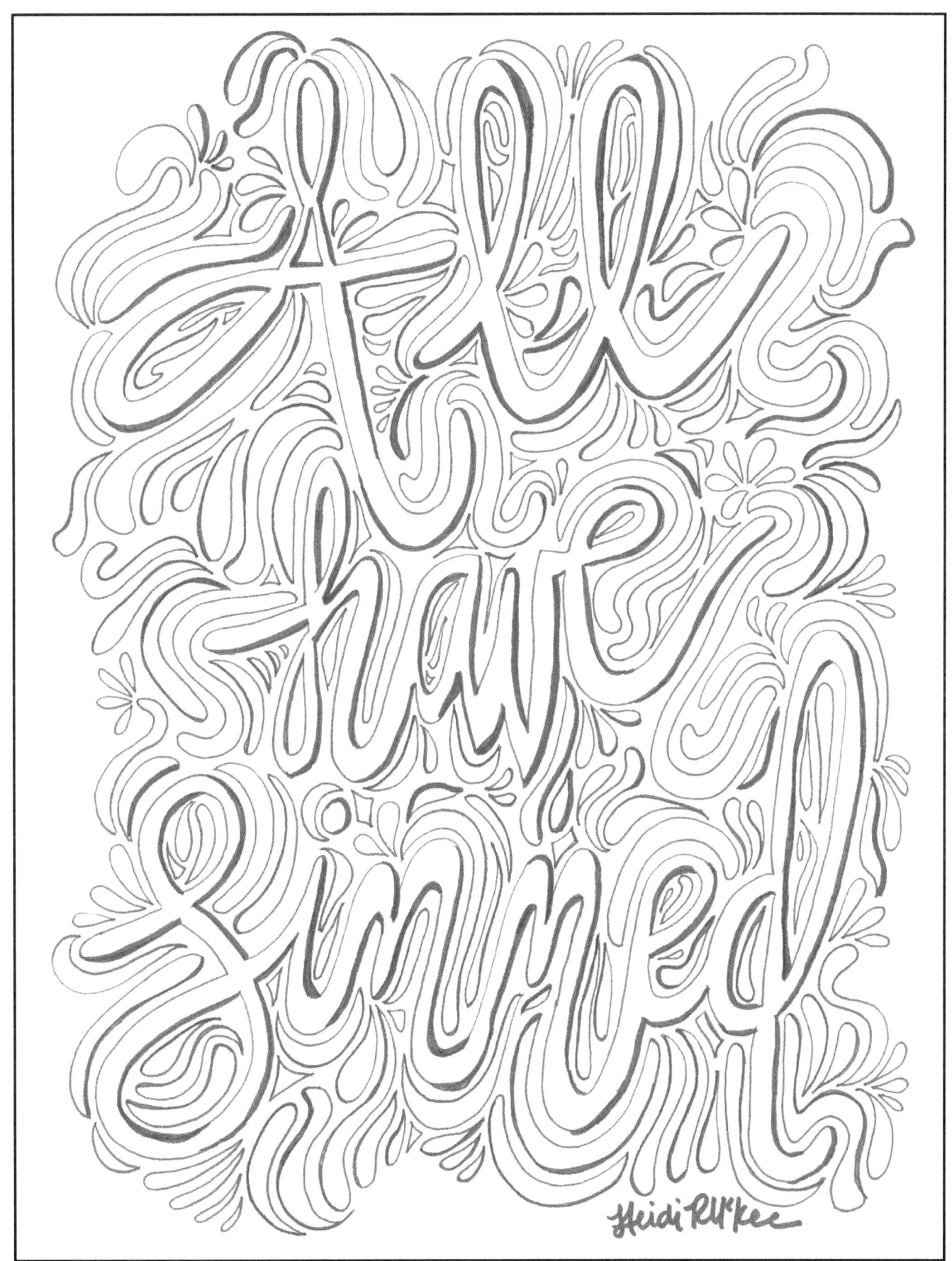

Every Knee Shall Bow
Philippians 2:10; Romans 14:11

What does "every knee shall bow" mean to you? Is it just more than the physical act of bending one's knees? I believe that "bowing" before God is a true act of worship. To humbly acknowledge how great the Lord is regardless of your physical ability or situation is true worship. We can bow our bodies, our minds, and our hearts before the Lord at any moment. He is waiting.

Through my career, I have had the privilege of being with multiple people who were actively in the presence of the Lord. There are no words to truly describe the experiences but each experience left me changed and reinforced that God is who He says He is. The most impressionable moments were with individuals who were in two very different stages in their Christian walk.

One morning I was standing at the bedside of a sweet lady with whom I shared a birthday with, only 70+ years apart. She was in her final days on earth and had not spoken or been aware of her surroundings for a few days. Suddenly, she opened her eyes, lifted her head towards the corner of the room and began speaking, "Yes, Jesus! Yes, amen. Yes, amen." This went on for several minutes as I stood silently beside her bed with my head slightly bowed. She finally said, "Yes, Lord. I will see you in the morning. Yes, Jesus. Amen!" With that, she closed her eyes and did not speak again. The following morning, shortly after 7:00am, this sweet lady entered into the Lord's presence for eternity.

Even when Christians fall away from being in relationship with Christ, Jesus is there waiting. Hebrews 13:8 speaks of Jesus Christ being "the same yesterday, and today, and forever." He will wait for you to return and bow before his presence. He will grab your attention anyway that He can.

I had the privilege of caring for a man in his early 40's that had experienced a cardiac arrest prior to arriving at the hospital. After a lengthy resuscitation effort, he was moved to the ICU in very critical condition with a prognosis of probable death. Over the next several days, it became apparent that his neurological recovery would be devastating at best. Life support was eventually removed. Shortly thereafter, he began to whisper "Jesus, water" repeatedly. I swabbed his mouth numerous times during the last few hours of my shift, hoping to quench his thirst until he was more awake and his swallowing could be safely evaluated. When I returned to the hospital, after a few days off, I was surprised at his progress. I told him about how he was begging me for water and that I had sponge swabbed his mouth so many times, that we ran out of mouth swabs. He began crying and then sobbing. He proceeded to tell me that during his "time away" he was in the presence of Jesus at the watering well. He said that he fell and bowed at the feet of Jesus, begging him for water. Jesus swabbed his mouth with a sponge and told him "I am the living water. Drink from me and follow me." (John 4:14) My patient left the hospital both physically changed due to his cardiac arrest and spiritually changed from experiencing the presence of the Lord.

What do your encounters with the Lord look like? Are you in awe of His goodness and grace or are you stationary without direction, wondering what He can do for you? Spend some time with your Savior. He is your lion and your lamb. He is waiting.

"So that at the name of Jesus, every knee shall bow.." Philippians 2:10
Mary Ann Mardis

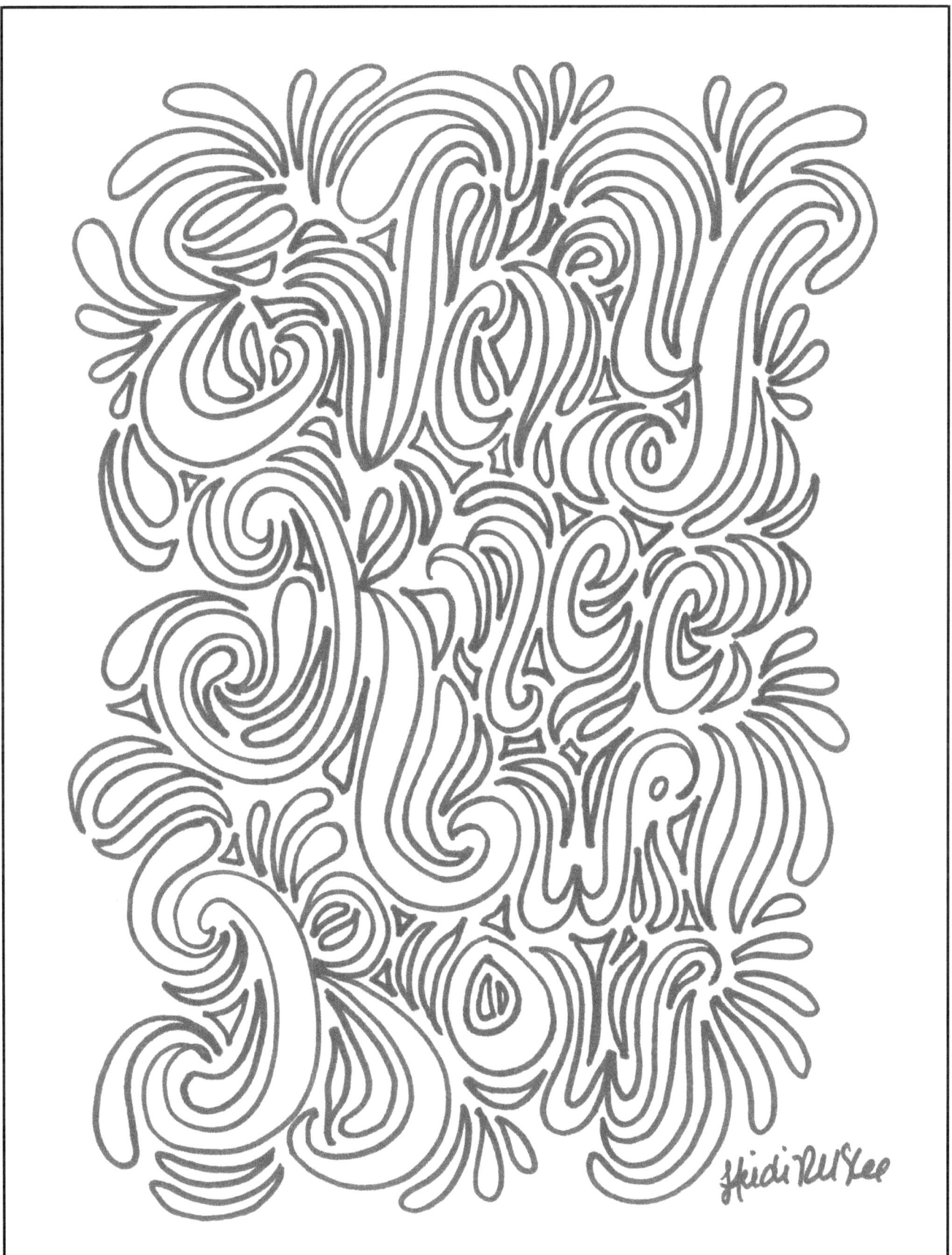

He Restores My Soul
Psalm 23

Have you ever felt as though you just cannot bear the weight anymore? You know the feeling, when all the little things pile up. Stuff that normally would not get to you, push you over the edge after days and days of little things building. Then BOOM- the dam breaks and you lose it. Maybe a traffic ticket when you're running late, someone in your house finally caught that virus that's been going around, or you go to start your car to take your kids to school and your battery is dead!

I love that God's word breathes life right into our hearts. The word of God brings comfort and a glimpse of the One who truly wants to restore us to normal—whatever that may be.

When my kids were between the ages of 1-6, I was exhausted, run down and empty. The demands of mothering four young kids had me in a dangerous place. I had no where to turn but to the source of peace Himself. Out of desperation I cried out to the Lord and found life in His word. Philippians 4:4-7 became the place I found restoration. Much like David in Psalm 23 I found rest in the *Giver of Life* and found wholeness in Jesus, the One who restores me.

> "The Lord is my shepherd, I lack nothing.
> He makes me lie down in green pastures,
> he leads me beside quiet waters, he restores my soul.
> He guides me along the right paths
> for his name's sake.
> Even though I walk through the darkest valley,
> I will fear no evil, or you are with me;
> your rod and your staff, they comfort me."
> Psalm 23

Tammy White

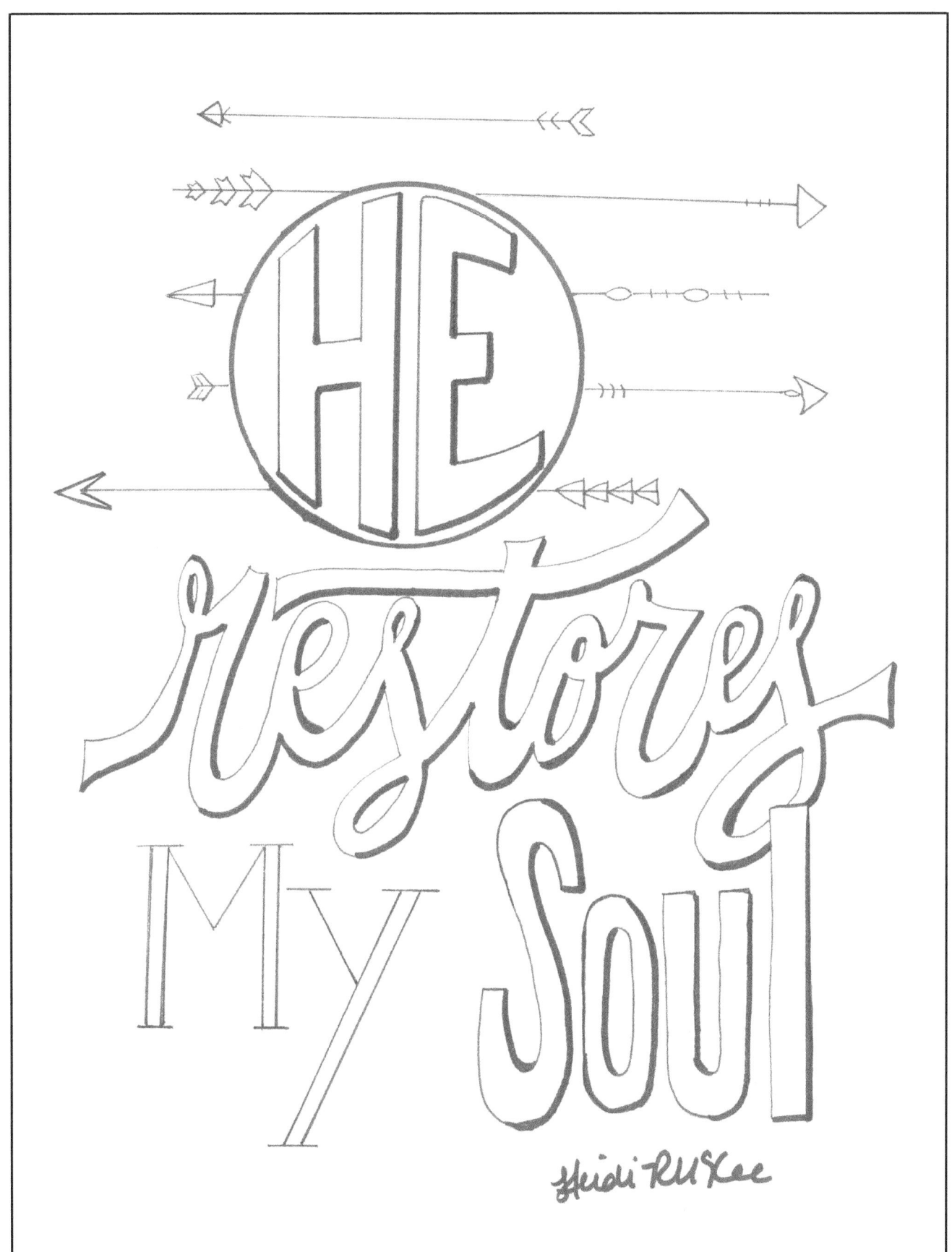

I WILL NEVER LEAVE YOU
Deuteronomy 31:8

Since knowing the Lord and accepting Him as my Savior I can only really remember a handful of times when I have felt utterly lost and alone. Once was when I was a young believer and a very hormonal teenager. I struggled with my own sin of greediness, selfishness and twisted self-perception. The lies of Anorexia and Bulimia* flooded into my soul and I believed them-- hook, line and sinker. "Your value is in your looks," "All you need to do is throw up after you eat and you'll never gain weight," and "You can be in control of your life!" God's truth that I was His loving creation was in battle with the lies of the world. These lies told me that my value came from how I looked.

Through a series of small steps, I eventually found myself down a very dark path of guilt, shame, and self loathing. It was in this state when I sank to my first lowest moment. One night alone in my room, I ate an entire box of chocolate bars that was meant to be sold for a school fundraiser. I tried vomiting, but it was just too much. I was sick, lost, angry, and ashamed. I laid in my bed and cried at how disgusted I felt and looked.

Suddenly, out of nowhere, I heard a deep and soft voice say, "My Goodness." I instantly felt the presence of God and tears rolled down my cheeks. Somehow deep inside I knew He was reminding me that He would never leave me and that He cherished me. But at the same time, I understood that my behavior was an abuse of His goodness. I felt trapped in my mind on how to relate with food. This 'love hunger' disease had poisoned my thinking. My secret of sneaking food, using laxatives, binging, and purging was hidden from all around me except my God. He reached deep down into my heart and massaged it with two painful, yet powerful words. In that very instant he reminded me that I was not alone.

His promise "I will never leave you or forsake you" has washed over my soul many times since that shameful night, turning my sin and shame into forgiveness and grace. When you feel despair and loneliness, know that the One who created you is there. He is able. He will not forsake you. He will never leave you. And remember that you are dearly loved by your Creator.

Tammy Grinn
grinn.org

*If you are struggling with a love hunger, do not wait to get help. The sooner you can get on the road to recovery the better off you will be. Start with reading <u>Love Hunger: Recovery from Food Addiction</u> by Dr. Fank Minirth, Dr. Paul Meier, Dr. Rober Hemfelt, Dr. Sharon Sneed, and Don Hawkins. Next, find a group of people that are struggling with the same problem and start meeting with them. Remember you are not alone.

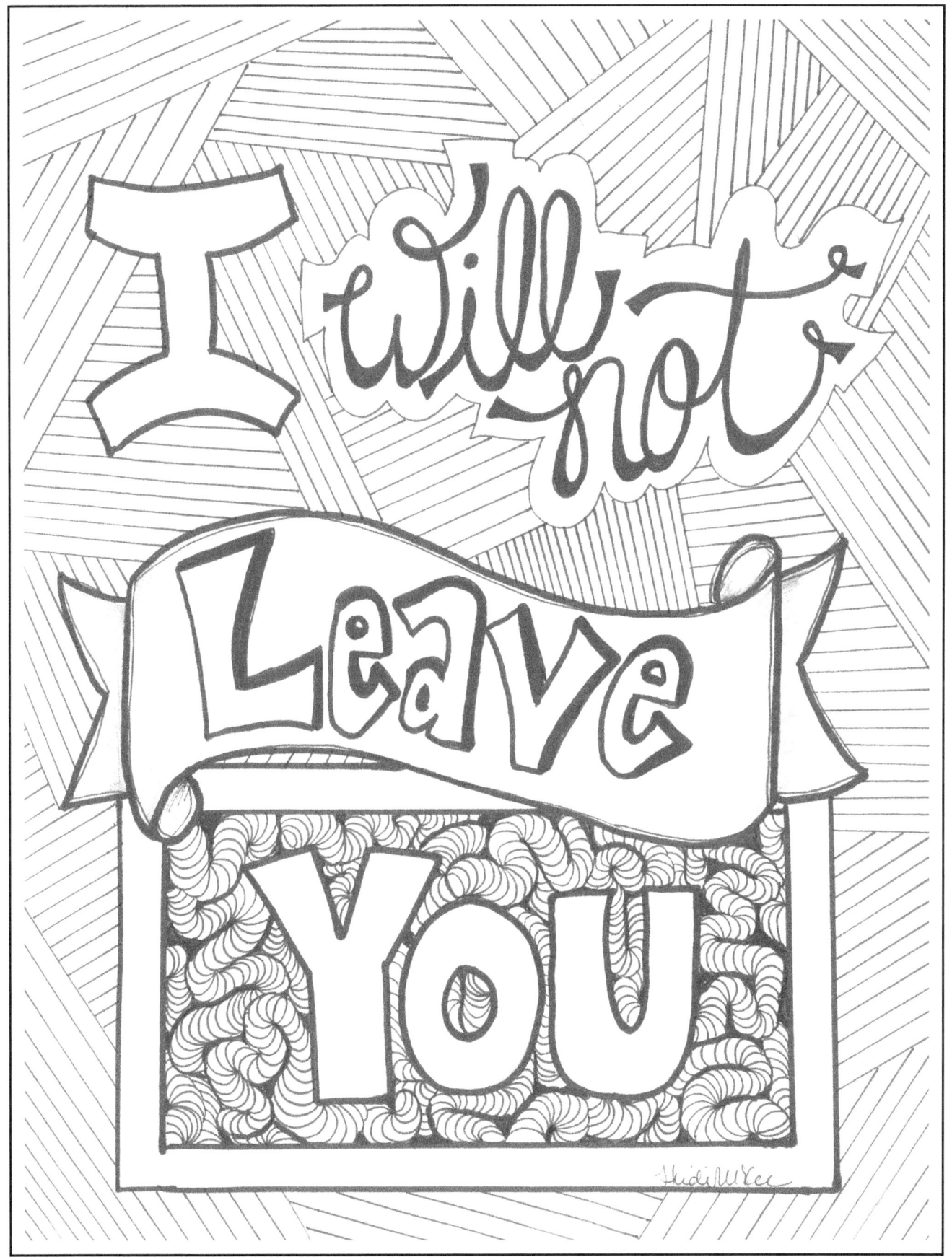

CHOOSE JOY
Galatians 5:22

Choosing joy in a world full of animosity is sometimes difficult. It takes a predetermined mindset focused on positivity before you find yourself in a room full of "negative Nellies." The realization that it is an actual "fruit" of the spirit listed in Galatians, gives a glimpse of God's will for us. God's will for us is to walk in His Spirit so that His joy can shine in and through us. To seek ways of being full of God's joy may be finding ways to use your gift He has blessed you with!

Choosing joy for me means serving my family. How to do that when they are so very busy, is a challenge at times. As a grandmother, I have made a commitment to serve Sunday dinner. It has become a joy!! To see those sweet faces gather around the table and share some of the most important things in life has become a real "joy" or blessing for me! My husband and I try to make it a time of blessing to compare with the busy stresses all the kids and grandkids are under! We try to add some activities with the dinner to make it fun and interesting for the entire family. Sometimes we even learn about a foreign country and serve food from that country and also have themed trivia questions! It makes for a fun atmosphere for all, while learning something new!!

If you have an opportunity to serve, try and bless someone! It will be a joy for those you serve and a blessing for you! Maybe you could send a card to a friend who is down? Or possibly call someone who is living alone? f you start thinking of ways to be a blessing, God will flood your heart with joy and your calendar will be full of opportunities to serve!

Karen Klein

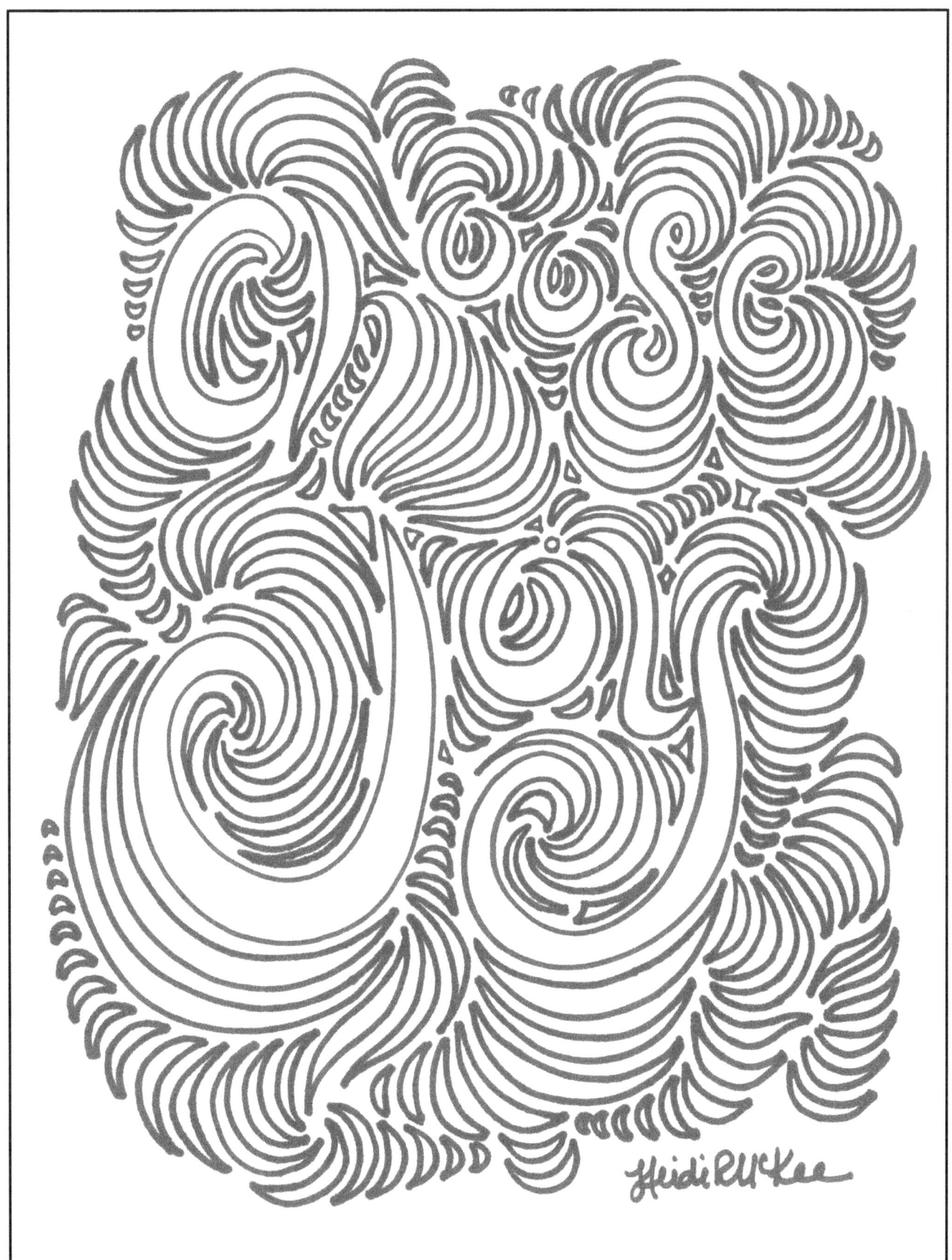

Put on the New Self
Col. 3:5-10

I spent the better part of my youth playing baseball. With that came a lot of time outside running around dirty baseball fields and feeling like I had more dirt on me than was left on the field. Then I would get home, and even now, I can still hear the marching orders of my mom telling me to get into the bathroom and get cleaned up. It was the dirty "S" word for any boy....SHOWER! But often it wasn't the shower that was the problem. It was what took place after the shower that got my mom really going. After getting all nice and clean I did the unthinkable. Yep. You guessed it...or maybe not. I put my dirty clothes...including underwear...back on. I mean seriously!!! Who does that kind of thing? Obviously I did.

But as a believer in Christ I find that I have something equally as troubling that takes place in my life. God instructs us to *"take off your old self with its practices and put on the new self, which is being renewed in knowledge in the image of its Creator."* (Col. 3:9-10) All of that dirty, filthy sin that was part of the "old self/nature" we are called to do away with. We have been "washed" by the blood of the Lamb and our lives should reflect that, not that of the "old" self. I think any of us would think it is disgusting to even think about taking a shower and then turn around and put the same smelly, dirty clothes back on we had on before. How much more "disgusting" to have a new life in Christ and then turn around and put back on the same yucky, sinful "clothes" we once wore. I mean seriously! Who does that kind of thing? Obviously I have. Father, forgive me...(and I probably should have said that quite a few times to my mom too).

Marty McKee

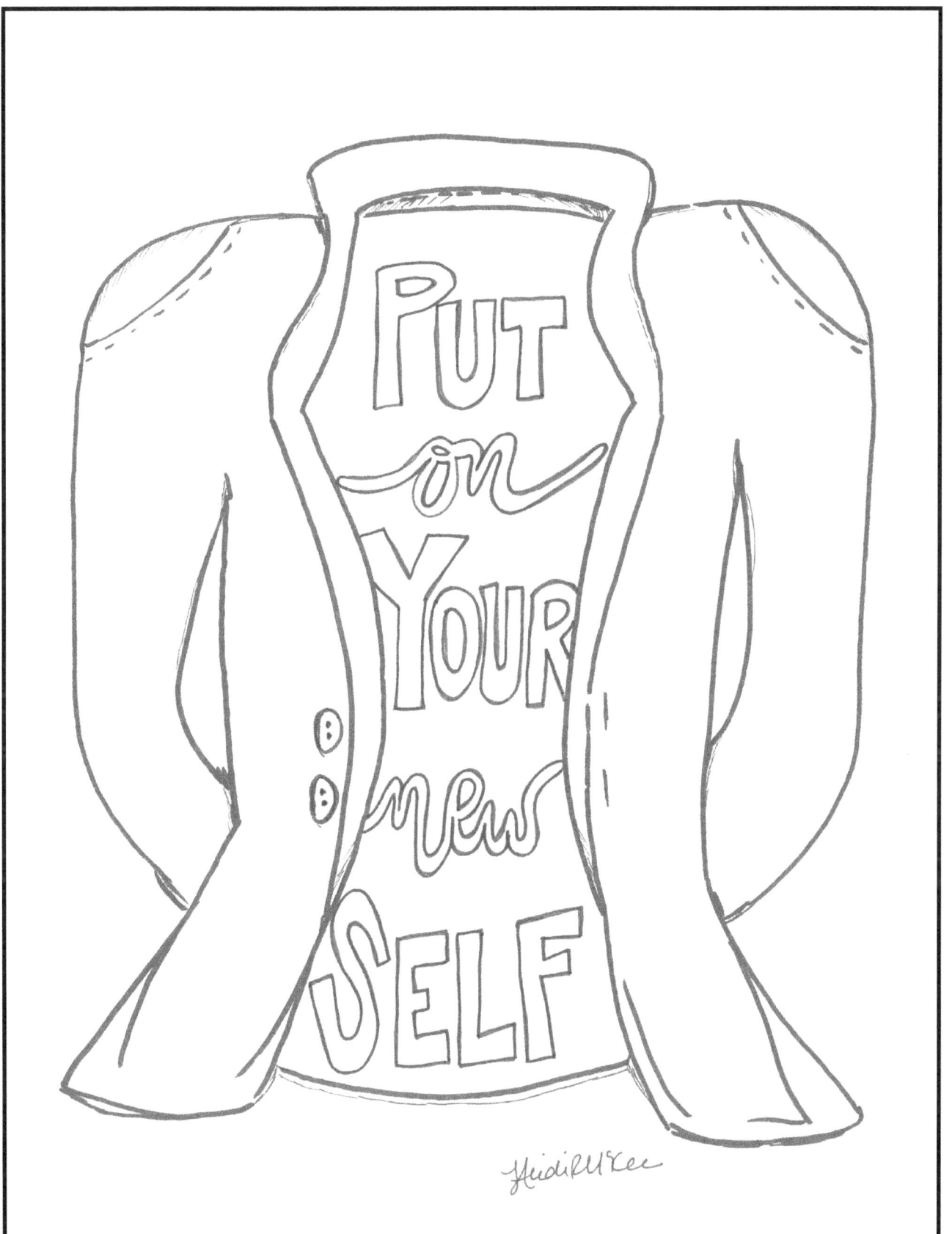

God is Light
John 8:12

Several years ago I lived with some friends on their 24 acre farm out in the country. While they were away on a vacation I decided I wanted to help them out and have all of the property around the house mowed before they got home. When I say "property" we are talking several acres and several hours of work outside. Luckily it was a beautiful day and I even took my shirt off to get a fresh tan. My friends returned a couple of days later and to my surprise one of the first things they said to me was, "Wow, you've spent some time in the sun lately haven't you?" The evidence of my labor (and the sun) was seen in my sunburn that was still glowing two whole days later.

I've thought about that moment several times over the years. Not only at moments when I've endured a nasty sunburn but more so wondering if people would look at me as a follower of Jesus and share those same words. Would someone look at you or me and say, "Wow, you've spent some time with the Son (Jesus) lately haven't you?" It is evident! By your actions. By your words. By your relationships. And it is a direct result of being in the SONlight. Maybe my question to all of us should be, "How much time have you spent in the SONlight lately?" If it is anything like my time mowing in the sun that day people will notice by your life that you have been basking in the light of the Son!

Marty McKee

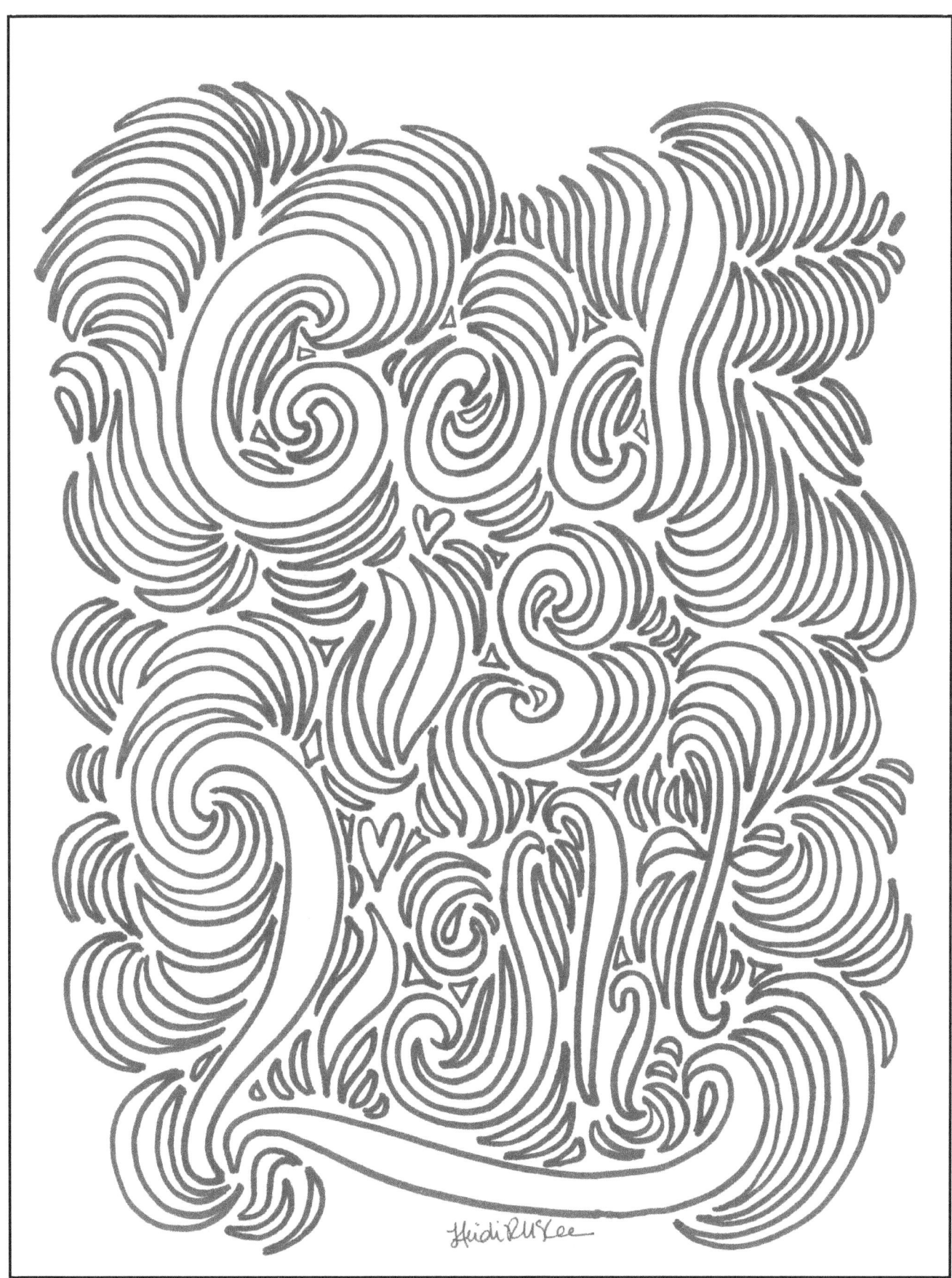

We Love Because He First Loved Us
1 John 4:19

In January 2013 my sister became a mom for the first time to three amazing teenagers. After an almost three-year spiritual, emotional, and financial battle to legally call them their own, I decided to board a plane and fly across the ocean to see them! My sister and brother-in-law were serving as missionaries when God finally made them parents. Of course Auntie Heidi had to meet them!

My flight got in really late, and my niece and two nephews were not there to greet me at the airport (bummer). My sister had waited 13 years for these babies, she was going to start them on great sleeping schedules, although they were 14, 15 and 16 years of age. When we got to their house, she told me I could go upstairs and hug them. The minute I opened the bedroom door this angel sat straight up and even in the dark I could see her perfectly-white giant smile. IT WAS IMMEDIATE LOVE. I cannot describe it. My heart literally leapt out of my chest and I knew I was the aunt that would cry with her when that boy breaks her heart, that will eat chocolate and watch movies, that will take her shopping and buy her anything she wanted. It was indescribable. She wrapped her arms around me and said in a very thick Russian accent "Good Morning". (she meant 'Good Night' and I was smitten). And that exact scenario happened twice more with my nephews.

Tammy and Matt have adopted five kids from the Ukraine. They felt led to give these kids homes and they did what it took to do so! Was it easy? Was it cheap? Was it fun? No, heck no, and no! They simply sacrificed because they LOVED!

God did that. He sacrificed his only Son because of His love for us. Was is easy? Nope! Was it cheap? Cost a life! And you know it was not fun! He did it out of LOVE. "For God so loved the world…"

We have the capacity to love because of the love he showed us! When we realize what an amazing sacrificial love that is, we will love more unconditionally and with more passion.

Heidi McKee
Heidimckeeministries.com

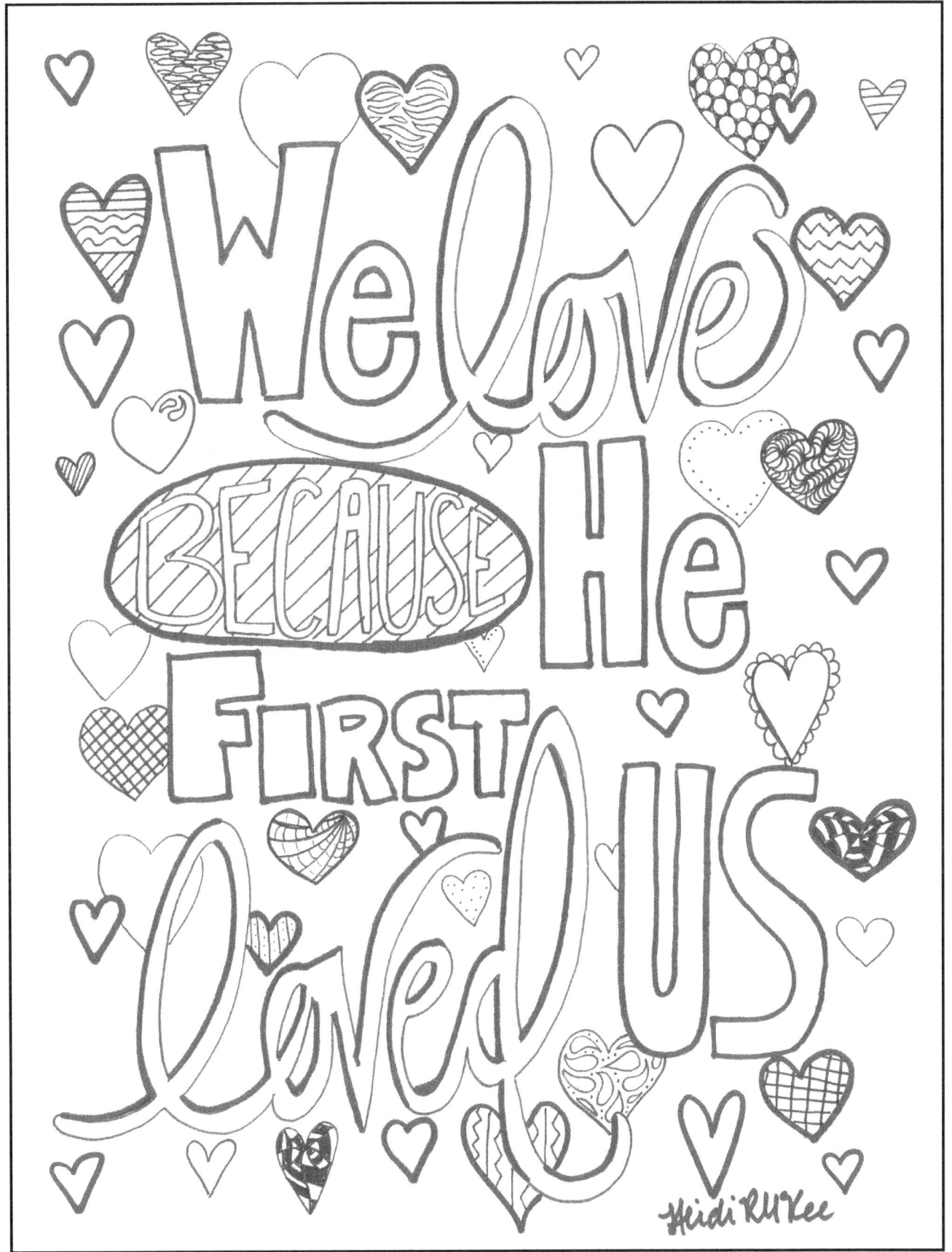

Pray Without Ceasing
1 Thessalonians 5:17

Let's face it! A regular prayer time is priceless, and almost impossible. For some reason it's the only life line we have yet EVERYTHING else jumps in front and takes priority. YEARS ago I recognized that I am the ONLY momma that will pray for my kids like a momma would...and IF I DON'T, then no one would! SO I came up with a little system to make sure I covered my kiddos in prayer everyday of the week (Even if it's just a quick one breath prayer). This has evolved, and now my kids and I pray together for these things over them! POWERFUL! Maybe use this to start your daily prayer schedule so that you can pray without ceasing too!

--Heidi McKee

Sunday- Salvation   Psalm 119:41-44 Rom. 10:13

Monday-Marriages, Mates, Purity Galatians 5:19-24

Tuesday- Teachers, Coaches, Administrators   James 3:1-2; Psalm 111:10

Wednesday- Wellness & Health Jer. 17:14

Thursday- Thirst for God's Word and Righteousness

Psalm 63:1; Psalm 42:1-2; Matt. 5:6

Friday- Friends, Faith & Fellowship   Romans 12:2

Saturday- Celebrating Answered Prayer

Secured Promises!   John 16:23-24, Matt 21:22, 1 John 5:14-15

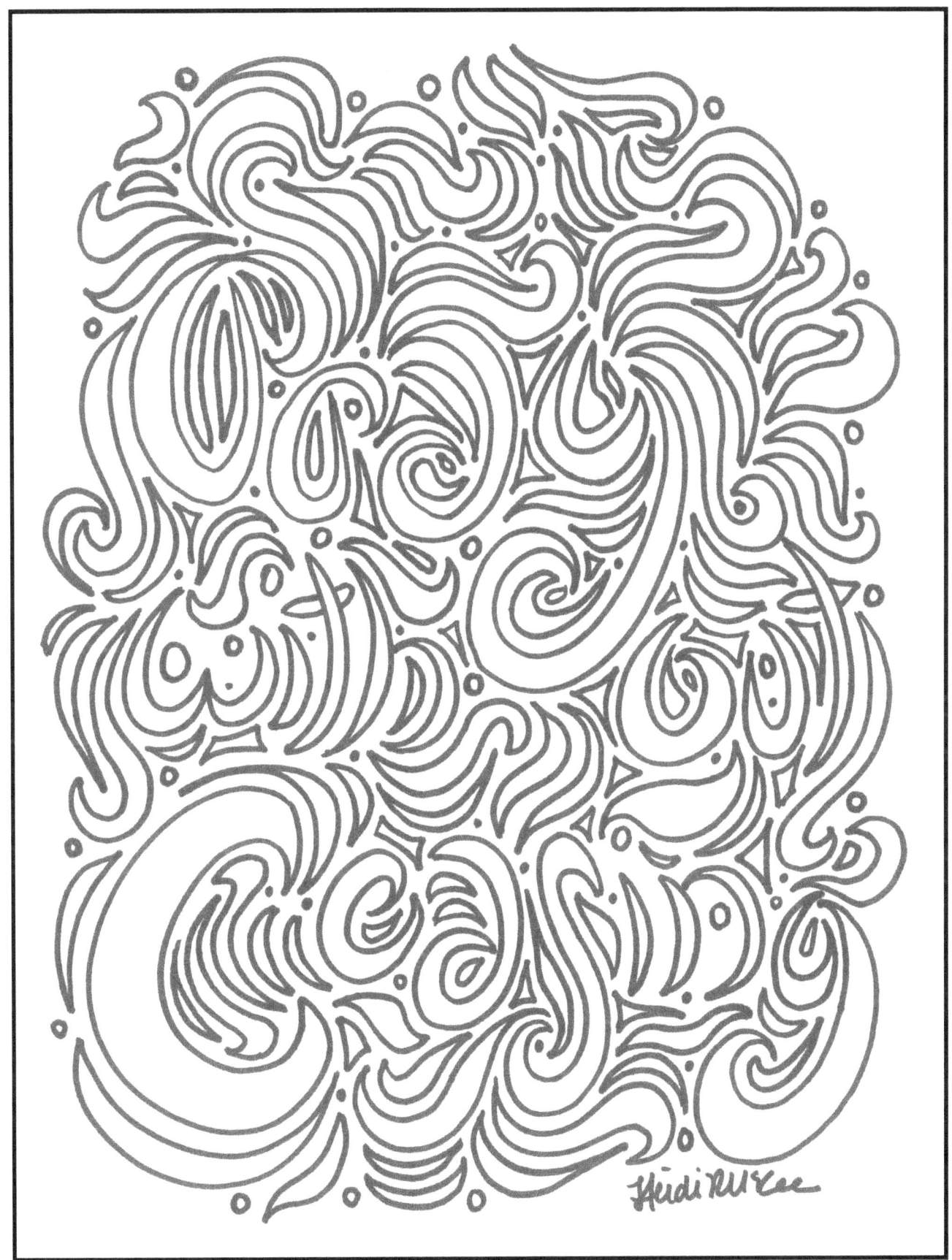

Abide In Me
John 15:5

The other night I sat down to my computer to do some work. The silly thing would not turn on. I was frazzled and worried SICK that I had lost every file, photo, and application because of a crashed computer. I called Apple to see how I can trouble shoot. I was a hot mess.

"Ma'am, calm down, let's start at the beginning. Is the computer plugged in?"

Silence.

How embarrassing! I was frantically pushing the power button, holding it down, jumping all around, yet I never checked the power outlet. The plug had somehow been removed from the wall. It worked perfectly once it was plugged in.

Truth is, that is how we are with Christ. We go through our day powerless because we had not plugged into *the* major power source-Jesus Himself. Apart from Him we can do nothing- just like my computer was worthless without the surge of power.

Jesus calls Himself the vine and we are the branches. We will bear no fruit if we are separated from Him. We need to Abide, or Plug in to Him each day so that we can actually have power to survive the day. Next time you are wondering how you will make it, try plugging in the Power Source- become the branch so you can produce fruit! He is there waiting.

"Jesus said "Abide in Me, and I in you. As the branch cannot bear fruit of itself unless it abides in the vine, so neither can you unless you abide in Me. I am the vine, you are the branches; he who abides in Me and I in him, he bears much fruit, for apart from Me you can do nothing."
John 15:15

Heidi McKee
Heidimckeeministries.com

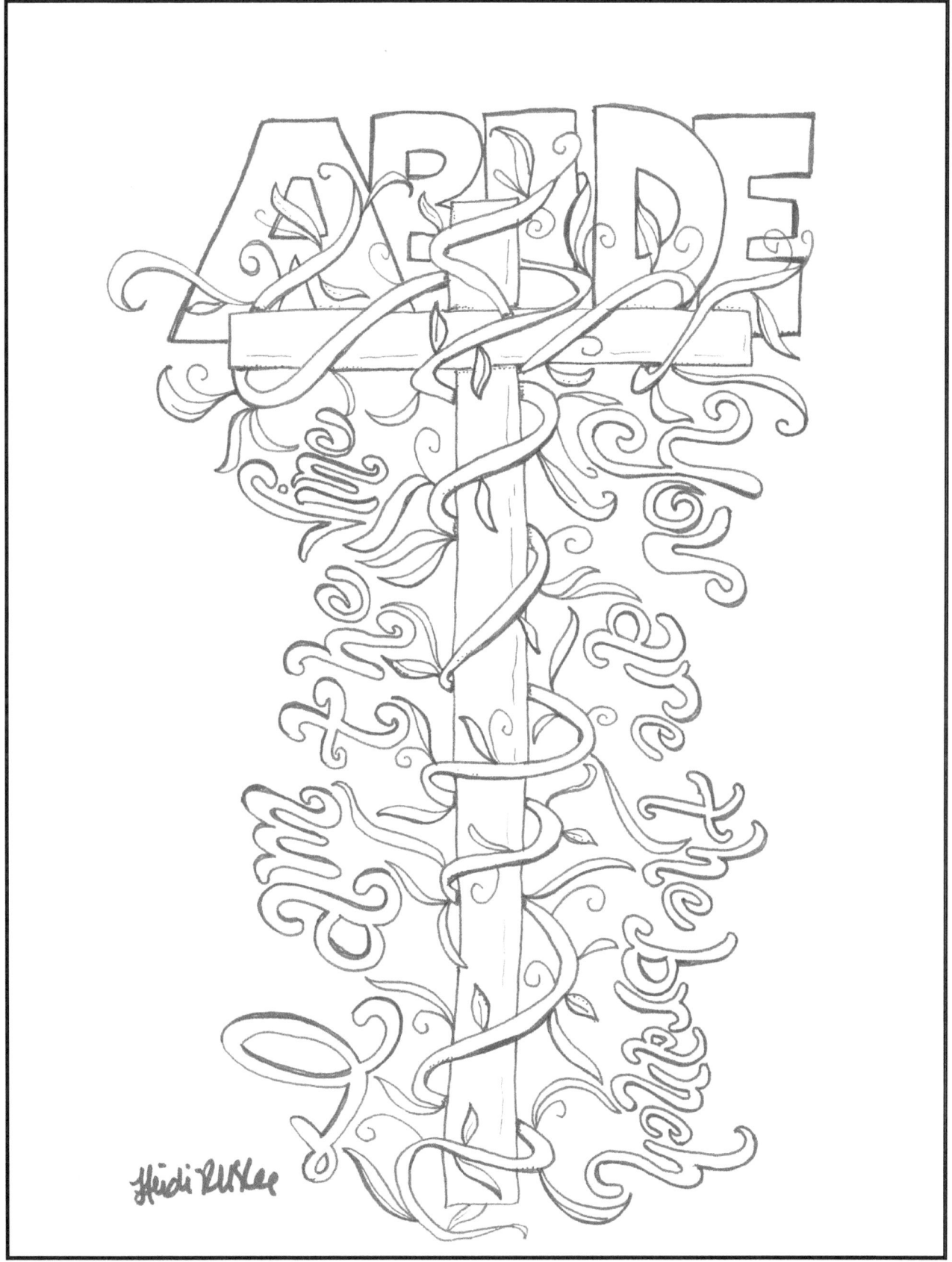

God is our Refuge
Psalm 91

Do you ever forget or take for granted just how big our God is? Do you limit God and his abilities? Are you ever amazed by the ways God reminds us that we are His children and He is with us at all times?

Recently, my family experienced God's protection and deliverance from trouble. My husband and I have six amazing children who love the Lord. A few weeks ago our 18-year old daughter, Payton, left to go to her friend's house. Within a few short minutes we heard a frantic pounding on the front door. We could not have been prepared for what we saw as we cautiously opened it. On the other side of the doorway stood our daughter covered in blood. My mind raced with questions! " What is wrong? What happened to you? Where is the blood coming from? Were you attacked?" Unfortunately, we could not get answers from her. In an instant, it became apparent she could not speak anymore, she was only able to say a garbled "VAAAAAAAAD"(she was trying to say bad) … Our family raced to get towels as we all feared the worst. In a few short moments it was crystal clear that we must get her to the hospital.

The five minute drive is a blur, however, I do recall hysterically crying out to the Lord," God please protect Payton, our baby girl." I frantically called my best friend asking her to pray. I called out to the Lord that the ER would be empty (not a likely scenario on a weekend night). I prayed for the doctors who would be treating our daughter and I prayed for total and complete healing.

Upon our arrival at the ER, I hysterically ran inside. Praise God, there was not one person in the waiting room, except for the security guard. I screamed through my tears begging for her help. At this point, she was shaking uncontrollably and unable to communicate without slurring and drooling. They rushed my daughter to the nurses station. My best friend appeared within minutes. She began reading Psalm 91 out loud over my daughter. "I will say to the Lord, my refuge and my fortress, my God, in whom I trust. For it is He who delivers you from the snare of the trapper."

Within minutes we were rushed into the CT scan, while the doctors made plans for care flight, anticipating the worst. I began singing "Amazing Grace" and "Jesus loves me" in hopes of soothing her failing body and mind. Another family friend, Dr. Jim, appeared in the hallway, explaining that our 11 year old called him (my mom heart melted). Dr. Jim immediately began praying over each specific vessel of her head and body. Over the course of 5 hours, we remained in the ER hallway- in full view of everyone. They could have isolated us in a room, but then people would not be able to see God at work! My prayer warriors never ceased. At one point, the ER doctor said "Whatever you are doing, keep it up, it is working." Praying- calling out to God, our Father, crying out for deliverance from the present trouble we were facing is what we were doing, trusting in Him. And then, it happened—every test came back negative!

Four and a half hours after our arrival, our daughter finally woke up. She spoke clearly and was actually worried the blood would not come out of her new jeans! I cannot express the elation upon hearing her sweet voice produce these clear words. As we left the hospital with the simple diagnosis of a massive nose bleed, several nurses and the orderly said "God was with you tonight!" Yes! God showed up big and revealed to everyone in the ER that night that He is listening for His children's cry. He is our protector. He is our Refuge in times of trouble.

God desires to be our shelter and protector when we face danger or trouble. We simply need to call out to Him in trust. He will deliver us! God is our Refuge.

Mary Beth Nix

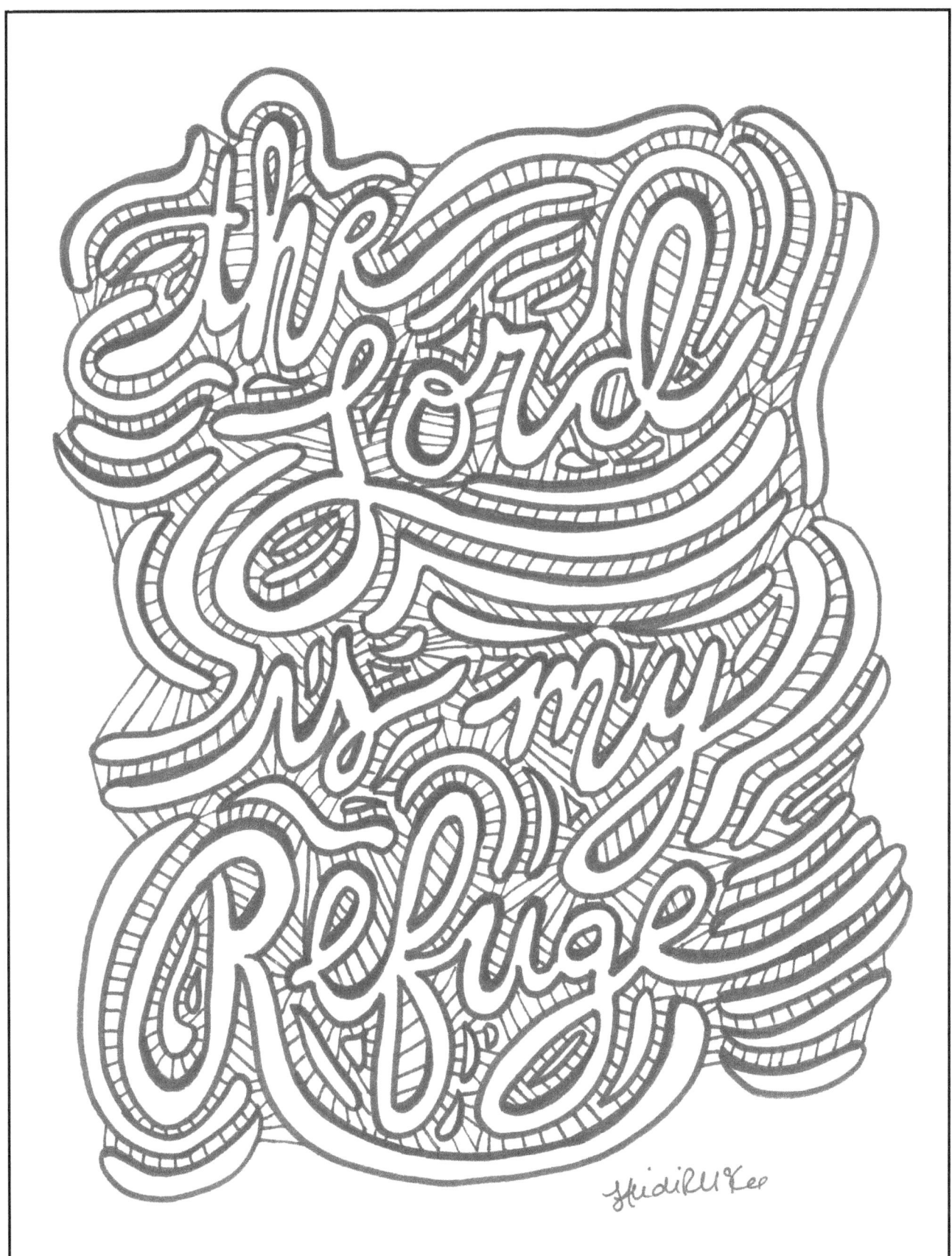

Give Thanks
1 Chronicles 16:34

Being a Dad has been one of the greatest joys of my life. However, along this journey I have learned that being a parent can be a very thankless job. I've watched as Heidi and I have served our kids tirelessly to make lunches, clean up messes, help with homework projects, take to sporting events, take to friends houses, and the list goes on and on and on and on...you get the point. If you are a fellow parent you know this list well too. And often after painstaking hours of service not even as much as a simple "Thanks" comes our way. Has any other parent ever endured this or is it just me?

I really don't say this to pick on my kids. Actually, as a follower of Jesus, I often find myself stuck in this same scenario. With all that God has done and continues to do for me...day in and day out...over and over and over and over...you get the point. Does He hear as much as a simple "Thanks" from me? You? As much as I seek to provide for my earthly kids how much more our Heavenly Father provides for you and me as His children. And if I think my children should be thankful for what I have done how much more should we GIVE THANKS for all that our Father has done and continues to do...over and over and over and over...I hope you get the point!

As you color this page, go through all the things you are grateful for! Give a heartfelt thanks to the one who has blessed you!

"Give thanks to the Lord, for he is good: his love endures forever."
1 Chronicles 16:34

Marty McKee

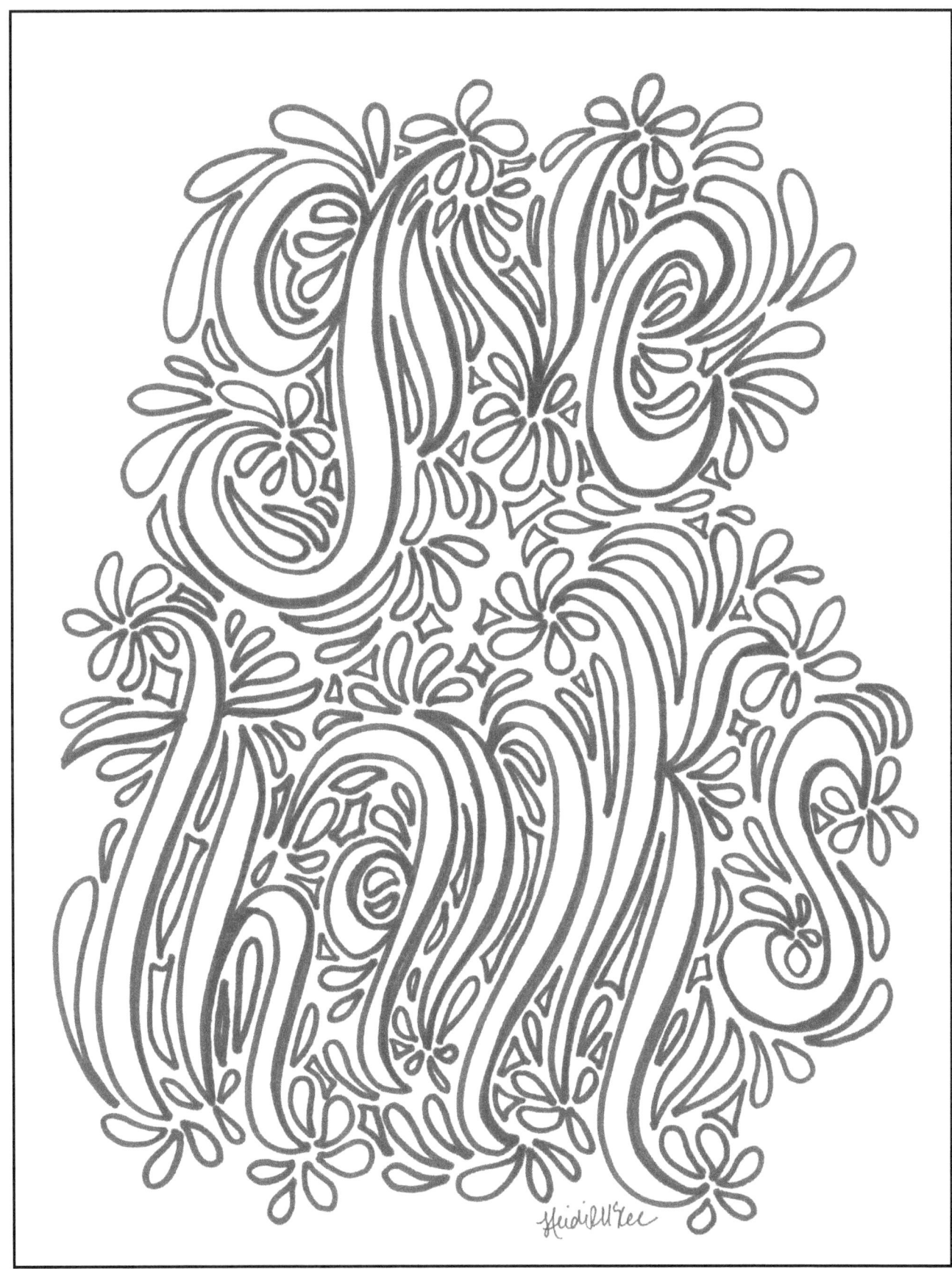

By Faith
Hebrews 11

One day I was driving and thinking-this is sometimes a dangerous thing. My mind started wondering about the idea of creation. I was questioning everything. How do we KNOW God made this world? What if we are just someone's dream and one day he'll wake up and we will cease to exist? What if everything I have been taught is just a hoax?

My mind spiraled into a vortex I didn't know existed. I asked God, "how do I know the truth?" Then Hebrews chapter 11 came to my mind. Faith, by definition "is confidence in what we hope for and assurance about what we do not see."

Truth is, there are a LOT of things that I don't see, but I believe in. I cannot see the wind in a storm, but I have confidence it is there. I do not see the love my mom has for me, but I have an assurance it's strong. The truth is, FAITH is what I have to have to continue stepping forward. "By faith we understand that the universe was formed at God's command, so that what is seen was not made out of what is visible." Hebrews 11:2

Often I tell my kids to "just trust me." I know what's best, and I implore them to "by faith" trust me. Same with the maker and creator of this universe! It is only by FAITH I will understand.

Next time you start questioning God's Amazing Grace, decide to believe BY FAITH- that's the only action you need to have confidence in!

Hebrews 11:39

Dear God, I am sorry my faith is weak sometimes. Forgive me for letting my mind wander into the deep dark-never coming back "what-ifs" of life! Help my faith be strong! Help others see my faith. Help me show others how to live 'by faith'. Thank you for faith and it is by faith we pray, Amen.

Heidi McKee
Heidimckeeministries.com

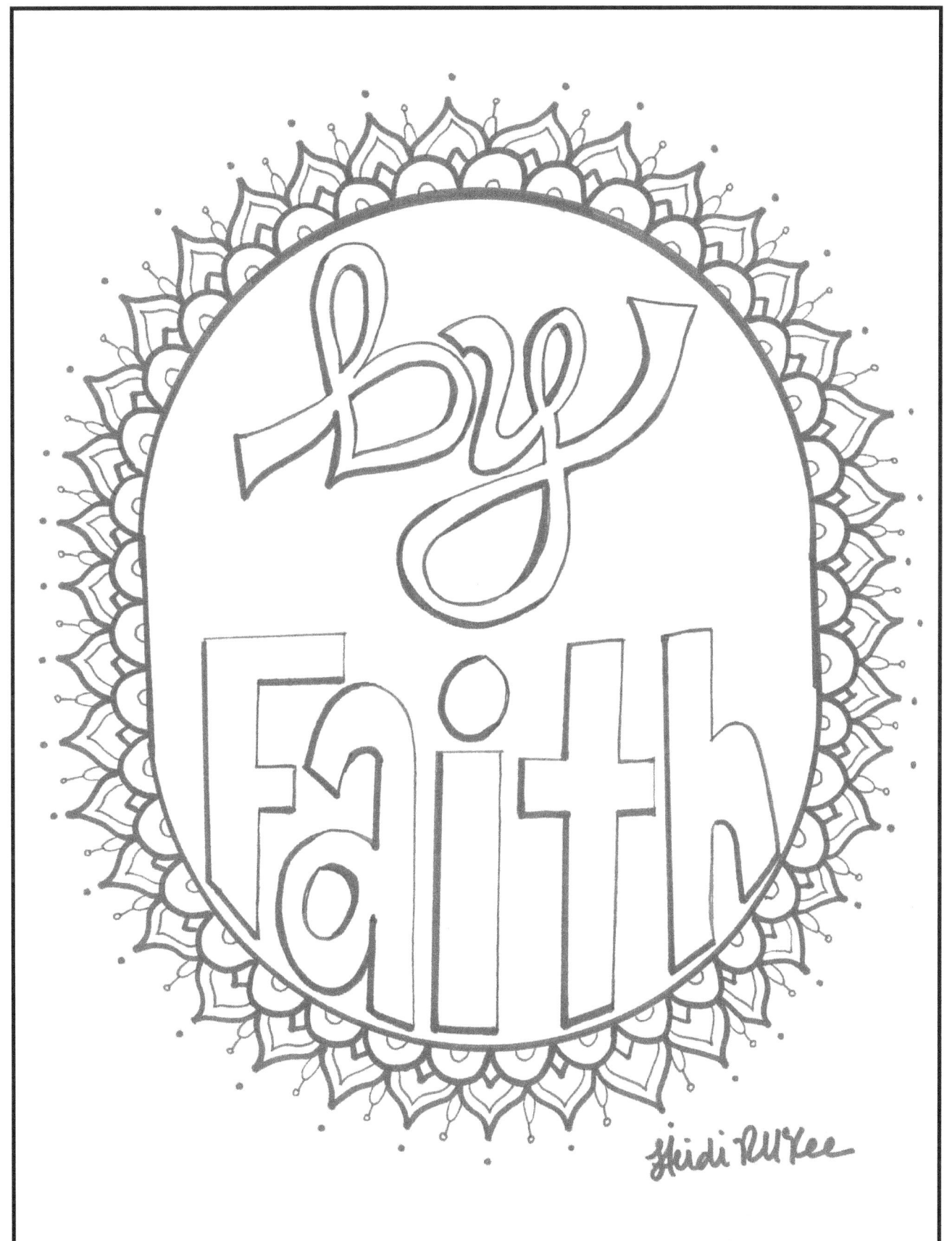

By Grace you have been Saved
Ephesians 2:8

Have you ever experienced a pardon? You totally deserved wrath, but for some reason was let off scot-free. Do you remember how that made you feel?

In college I drove a 1992 Candy Red Honda Prelude, decked out with sunroof and black leather seats. I loved that car. My parent's home was 81 miles down old highway 4 and if I timed it just right could make it home under an hour. That's if I didn't get pulled over. Yes, I was a speeder. One highway patrol pulled me over 3 months in a row. After the 3rd ticket, my court appearance would be in the tune of $1300! Might as well be a million to a starving college kid.

That Tuesday morning, I got dressed to meet the judge and throw myself on the mercy of the court. I had planned tears, a good story, and practiced my puppy-dog eyes. Three tickets and potential license suspension, this girl was a nervous wreck.

"Hi, my name is Heidi Klein, I am to appear in court for multiple, uhem, speeding tickets." I squeaked at the clerk. "Just a moment." She flatly said as she pounded the keys to her computer.

"What was your name again?"

"Heidi Klein." Sweat is now dotting my upper lip.

Typing and breathing loudly the court clerk peered over her glasses to me and said,--and I still cannot believe this happened--"Maam, there is no record of you or a court date, are you sure you were pulled over?" I handed her the citations and she reviewed. Punched the keys more. The people in line behind me started rocking back and forth.

"Nope, nothing here. You're free due to a technicality. Must be your lucky day."

Pretty sure I floated out of that court house and vowed to NEVER EVER speed again!

I deserved the slammer or a fine at least! I broke the law and I should've paid! But I was pardoned. I was given a second chance. I was shown grace.

How many times did I disrespect my parents? Or spoke shortly to my husband. I do deserve a harsh response, my action did warrant an unkind gesture, but I have always received grace.

"Undeserved favor is what Christ has shown us! For by grace you have been saved through faith. And this is not your own doing, it is the gift of God." You were offered a gift! Like a free "get out of jail card" or a "waived" speeding ticket, YOU have received a pardon from all the horrible things you have done! Christ has saved you- it is by GRACE! Accept it!

Heidi McKee
from the book *Find your Passionate Purpose: In Life, Leadership and Love*

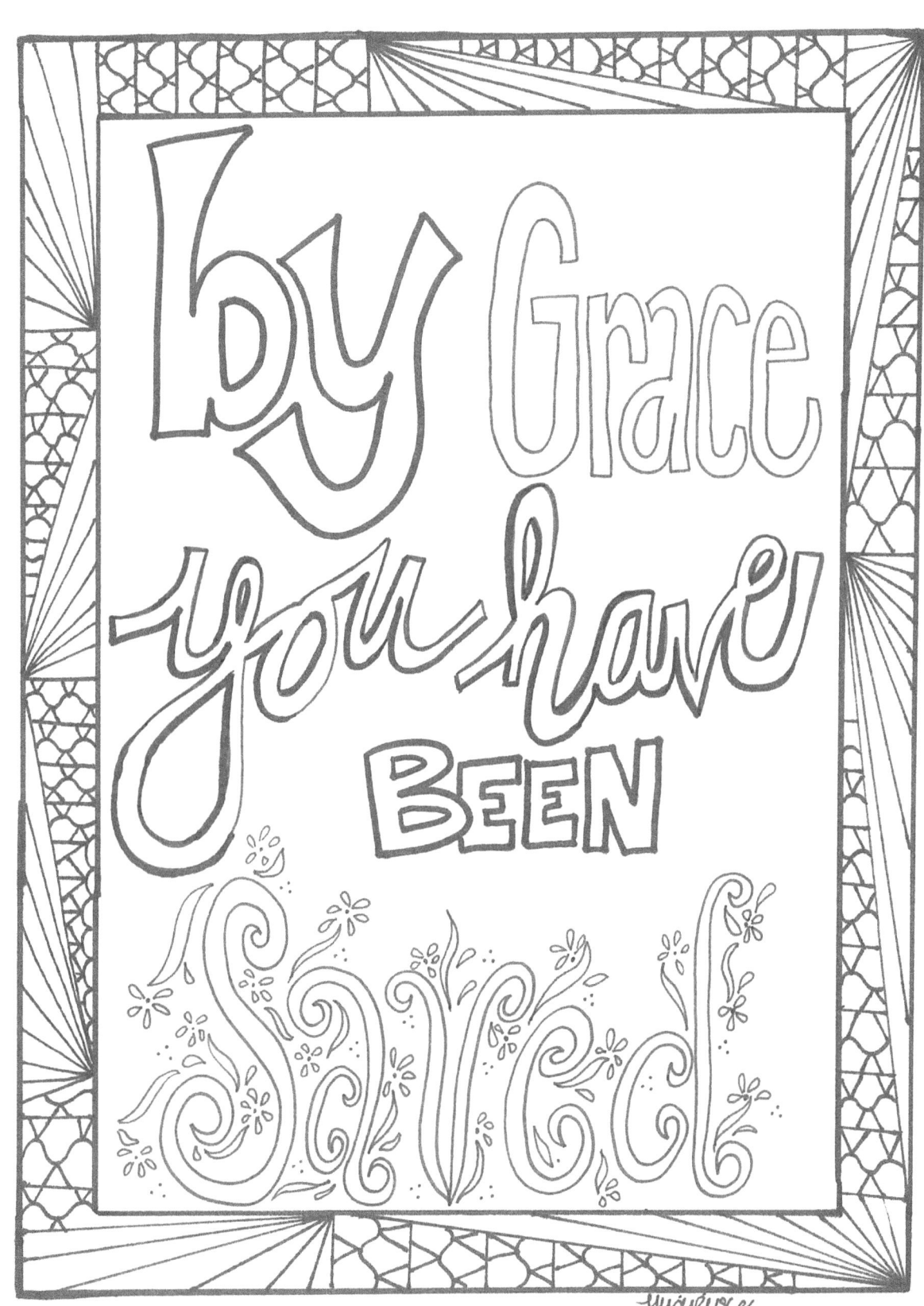

Be Joyful in Hope
Romans 12:12

Some days you peek out of the corner of your eye before you're able to lift your head off of that soft pillow. You just need to make sure that nothing is coming out of left field to whack you as you lift your achy body up out of bed for one more day.

That's the feeling I've had for the past few weeks. Not sure what's going on around here, but literally in one weeks' time the car broke down, the toilet leaked through the downstairs ceiling onto the wood floor, the sink faucet broke, the fence started falling down and our new son had his first Real 'American-I'm-finally-in-a-family' birthday! (He was recently adopted). The unusual thing is that in spite of all the recent highs and lows our family has experienced, we have managed to keep on grinning and bearing it. I mean, truthfully deep down there is still a genuine smile. If you are still long enough, you might even hear a faint sound resembling laughter.

The morning I walked down to the kitchen and noticed water splashing everywhere from the leak I wanted to scream! But for some reason, I kept my cool (mostly) and calmly walked over to the laundry room to grab some towels and a bucket. Shocking. Even my boys, who were in the distance, cautiously observing my every move, were surprised at my unnatural movements. And then my husband came down the stairs and shocked us all! He walked in like Mr. Enthusiasm, with a 'we can do this, no problem' attitude and says with a twinkle in his eye, "We'll get to that after church!" Um. Okay. I've decided that we are either A. delusional or B. finally starting to learn how to roll with life's blows with a bit of style and grace. The verdict's still out.

For now I plan to lean on the side of grace with a dash of crazy. Grit your teeth, lift your head, smile and keep on keeping on.

"Be joyful in hope, patient in affliction and faithful in prayer." Romans 12:12

Tammy Grinn
grinn.org

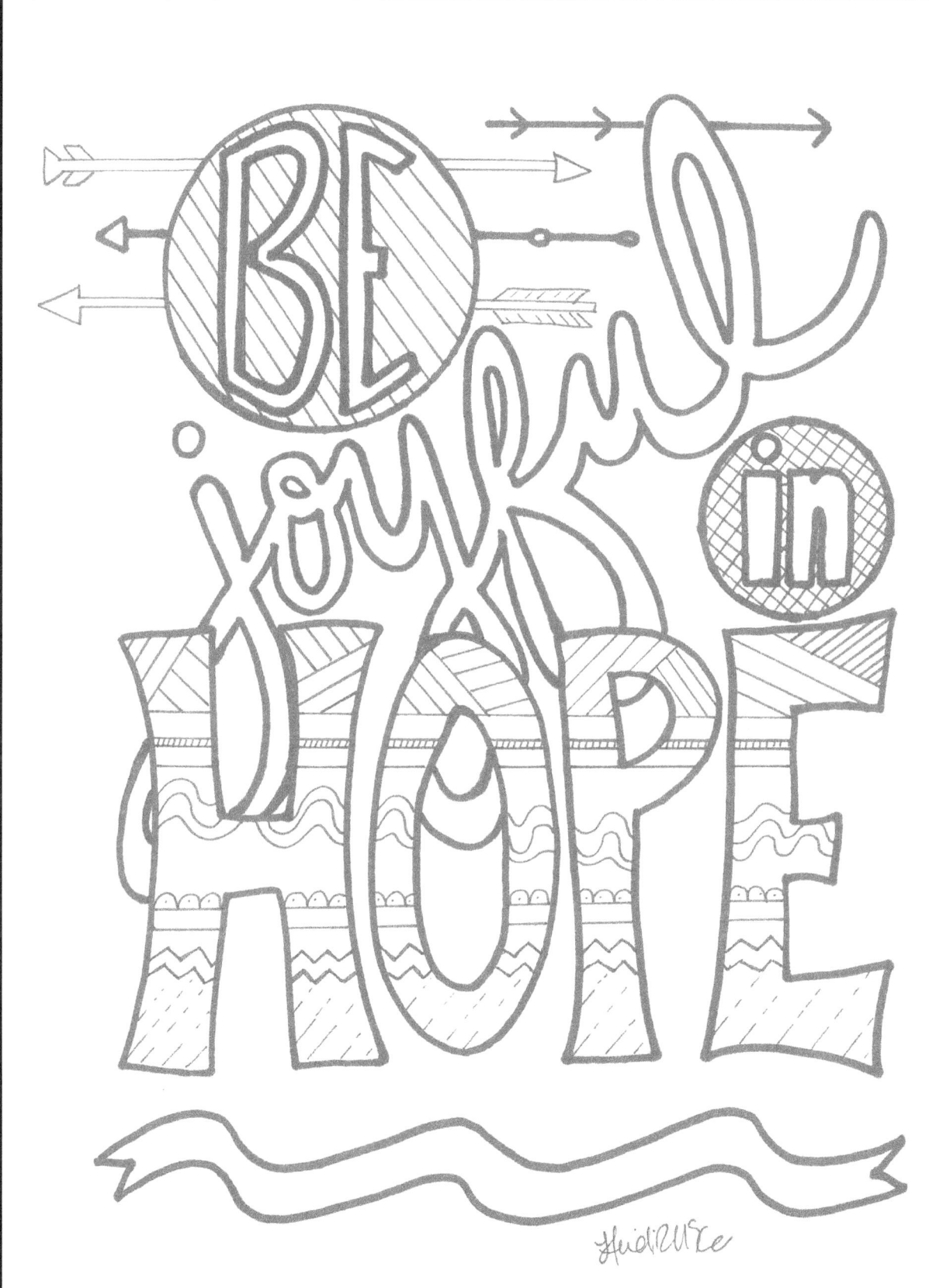